1/5/99

Grades 3-5

The Alaska Pipeline
Epcot Center
The Erie Canal
The Gateway Arch
The Grand Coulee Dam

The Hubble Space Telescope
The Lincoln Tunnel
Louisiana Superdome
The Sears Tower
The Seattle Space Needle

AMERICA'S TOP 10

CONSTRUCTION WONDERS

By
Tanya Lee Stone

Published by Blackbirch Press, Inc.
260 Amity Road
Woodbridge, CT 06525

©1998 Blackbirch Press, Inc.
First Edition

Printed in the USA

10 9 8 7 6 5 4 3 2 1

Library of Congress Cataloging-in-Publication Data

Stone, Tanya Lee
    America's top 10 construction wonders / by Tanya Lee Stone.
        p. cm.—(America's top 10)
    Includes bibliographical references and index.
    Summary: Introduces ten unique American constructions including the Sears Tower,
the Erie Canal, the Lincoln Tunnel, the Alaska pipeline, the Grand Coulee Dam, the
Louisiana Superdome, the Seattle Space Needle, the Hubble Space Telescope, the
Gateway Arch, and Disney's Epcot Center.
    ISBN 1-56711-195-5 (lib. bdg. : alk. paper)
    1. Engineering—United States—Juvenile literature. 2. Building—United States—Juvenile
literature.
[1. Engineering. 2. Building.] I. Title. II. Series.
TA149.S76 1998
624—dc21   97–3609
                                                                            CIP
                                                                            AC

B L A C K B I R C H   P R E S S ,   I N C .
W O O D B R I D G E ,   C O N N E C T I C U T

AMERICA'S TOP
10
CONSTRUCTION WONDERS

AK

CANADA

Alaska Pipeline

The Alaska Pipeline

The 800-mile-long Alaska Pipeline carries oil across the entire length of the state. It crosses steep mountains, raging rivers, and permafrost—a permanently frozen layer beneath the earth's surface. The line was constructed by the Alyeska Pipeline Service Company and was an extremely complicated building project.

In 1968, oil was found under the ground in Prudhoe Bay, on Alaska's northern coast. The pipeline was built to carry the oil from Prudhoe Bay to the port of Valdez. There, large ships would pick up the crude oil and take it to refineries in the "Lower 48" states.

Alyeska's first major construction problem involved crossing Alaska's permafrost. The heat from the pipeline could thaw the frozen ground, so Alyeska's engineers decided to elevate the pipeline where necessary. Special crossings were built so that the migration routes of native caribou would not be disturbed.

The pipe itself is 48 inches in diameter, and it is wrapped with 4 inches of insulation. The sections that did not need to be elevated were buried between 3 and 35 feet below ground. In addition to the pipeline, 10 pumping stations were built to keep the oil moving.

In 1977, on August 1, the first tanker left Valdez carrying oil that had been transported through the Alaska Pipeline. Over a million barrels flow through the pipeline every day. Since oil is a limited natural resource, we will eventually use up the oil in Alaska. Today, the search for new sources of oil continues.

Location: Alaska
Completed: June 1977
Length: 800 miles
Diameter of pipe: 48 inches
Amount of oil flowing through pipeline: 1.6 million barrels per day
Cost: $8 billion
Fun fact: More than 83,000 sections of pipe were welded together to make the pipeline.

Opposite page:
The Alaska Pipeline was built in a zigzag pattern, which helps the pipeline adjust to the changing temperature of the oil.

AMERICA'S TOP

10

CONSTRUCTION WONDERS

AL   GA

Atlantic
Ocean

FL

Gulf of Mexico

Epcot
Center

Epcot Center

On October 1, in 1982, the Experimental Prototype Community of Tomorrow (Epcot Center) opened at Disney World in Florida. Walt Disney, who produced many famous animated cartoons, had the idea for Epcot Center in 1966. He wanted people to think about how science affects the future, and he wanted them to appreciate the many cultures of the world. The 2 main parts of Epcot Center—Future World and World Showcase—demonstrate these ideas.

Construction began in October 1979. To build Epcot Center, workers moved 54 million tons of earth, and they used 16,000 tons of steel and 500,000 feet of lumber! The total cost of the project was $900 million.

Spaceship Earth, which is located at the entrance to Epcot Center, is one of the most amazing engineering feats at Disney World. It is built like a geodesic dome—a strong, dome-like structure that has a framework of triangular shapes. Spaceship Earth is a sphere, however, instead of a half-circle. It is the world's first geodesic sphere and the largest geodesic structure. The sphere weighs 15.5 million pounds. It is 180 feet high and 165 feet in diameter. There are 954 triangular panels that form the outside of the structure. It is supported by 6 steel legs that are sunk 100 feet into the ground. Inside, visitors to Spaceship Earth ride on a motorized track that winds around the sphere. Along the way, passengers view exhibits relating to the history of communications—from the first printing press to astronauts' communications from space.

Location: Florida
Opened: October 1, 1982
Area: 260 acres
Cost: $900 million
Fun fact: About 10,000 workers helped build Spaceship Earth.

Opposite page:
Spaceship Earth is the world's largest geodesic building.

AMERICA'S TOP

10

CONSTRUCTION WONDERS

CANADA

ME

VT

NH

Erie Canal

MA

NY

RI

CT

PA

NJ

The
Erie Canal

★ ★ ★ ★ ★ ★ ★ ★   ★ ★ ★ ★ ★ ★ ★

Building the Erie Canal—the longest canal in America—was an amazing accomplishment at a time when construction equipment was much less advanced than it is today. In the early 1800s, transporting people and goods was difficult. In order to travel westward from the East Coast, people had to cross the Appalachian Mountains, which run from Maine to Georgia. In 1807, a man named Jesse Hawley had the idea of building a canal, or human-made waterway. This would connect the Hudson River to Lake Erie—a distance of 363 miles! Westward travel, he said, would be easier by boat than by land.

In 1817, on July 4, a groundbreaking ceremony was held in Rome, New York. It took workers the next 8 years to complete the Erie Canal. Many obstacles, such as rocky ridges, huge trees, and muddy swamps, stood in the way.

Structures called "locks" were built to allow boats to be raised or lowered between sections of the canal that varied in depth. The double locks that raised and lowered boats over a 76-foot-high ridge in Lockport, New York, were especially impressive. In some places the canal had to be elevated above ground level. To solve this problem, engineers designed aqueducts—raised structures designed to carry water.

In 1820, a passenger boat traveled through the first completed section of the canal. Five and a half years later, on October 26 in 1825, the entire canal was open. It was a huge success. By 1836, more than 3,000 boats traveled back and forth regularly on the canal.

Location: New York State
Opened: October 26, 1825
Length: 363 miles
Width: 40 feet at top; 28 feet at bottom
Depth: 4 feet
Number of locks: 83
Number of aqueducts: 18
Cost: More than $7 million
Fun fact: To announce the departure of the first boat on the canal, cannons were fired along the length of the canal and down the Hudson River to New York City.

Opposite page:
A boat motors down the tree-lined Erie Canal.

AMERICA'S TOP
10
CONSTRUCTION WONDERS

IA
NE
IL
KS
Gateway Arch
MO
OK
AR
KY
TN

The
Gateway Arch

In the 1930s, a St. Louis lawyer named Luther Ely Smith had the idea of building a memorial to commemorate St. Louis's role as a gateway to the West in the 1800s. Because of money problems and World War II, however, it took 30 years for the Gateway Arch to be completed.

After the war, in 1947, a contest was held to design the memorial, which was won by the architect Eero Saarinen. To symbolize a gateway, he designed a steel arch in the shape of an upside-down catenary—the curve that is made by a chain when it is suspended loosely between 2 points.

For the foundation, about 26,000 tons of concrete were poured into two 60-foot-deep holes, and 252 steel supports were set into the concrete. Once the foundation was ready, sections of the steel arch were lifted by crane and put in place, one at a time. When the 2 legs of the arch reached 72 feet, special rigs called "creeper derricks" were made for each leg. They carried the cranes on platforms high into the air.

On October 28, in 1965, a crowd of people cheered as the last steel section of the arch was placed. A "tram" elevator was installed to take visitors to the top. Because of the curved shape of the arch, the tram had free-swinging compartments, much like the seats on a Ferris wheel!

Once the arch was completed, work began on the underground visitors center. The Gateway Arch was dedicated on May 25 in 1968. Its official name is the Jefferson National Expansion Memorial in honor of United States president Thomas Jefferson.

Location: St Louis, Missouri
Dedicated: May 25, 1968
Height: 630 feet
Weight: More than 16,000 tons
Designer: Eero Saarinen
Number of visitors: 4.5 million per year
Cost: $13 million
Fun fact: When the Mississippi River flooded in 1993, workers pumped more than 1,000 gallons of water per minute out of the visitors center.

Opposite page:
The graceful form of the Gateway Arch is reflected in the Mississippi River.

AMERICA'S TOP

10

CONSTRUCTION WONDERS

CANADA

WA Grand
Coulee
Dam

OR   ID

The
Grand Coulee Dam

★ ★ ★ ★ ★ ★ ★ ★ ★ ★ ★ ★ ★

The Grand Coulee Dam, in the state of Washington, is the largest producer of hydro-electricity in America and third-largest in the world. When it was begun, it was the largest concrete structure ever built. About 12 million cubic yards of concrete were used to construct the dam—enough concrete to build a sidewalk that circles the earth twice!

In 1933, on July 16, a crowd of 3,000 people watched as the first stake was driven into the site of the Grand Coulee Dam. The dam, which was built in 2 parts, uses the Columbia River as a source of electric power. The dam also irrigates the dry farmlands of the region.

Before the dam could be built, it was necessary to uncover the underlying rock for the foundation. Shovel operators scooped up 20,000 wheelbarrow-loads of dirt every 7 hours, dumping it onto the largest conveyor system ever made. This "river of dirt" traveled 1 mile to what is now Crescent Bay Lake.

In December 1935, the first concrete was poured. Once the base was finished, the dam's steel skeleton was built. More than 20,000 interlocking concrete columns were then installed. By December 1941, the spillway—the area where water flows down a vast wall—was completed. Two power plants—one on each side of the spillway— were also finished. In 1967, construction of a third power plant was begun. The building of the Grand Coulee Dam was an extraordinary engineering feat. Even the spillway gates—the structures that allow the water to flow over the dam—were huge.

Location: Grand Coulee, Washington
Completed: December 31, 1941
Height: 550 feet
Length: 5,223 feet
Cost: $1 billion
Fun fact: The dam is about as high as a 46-story building.

Opposite page:
The enormous spillway gates are clearly visible in this aerial photo of the Grand Coulee Dam.

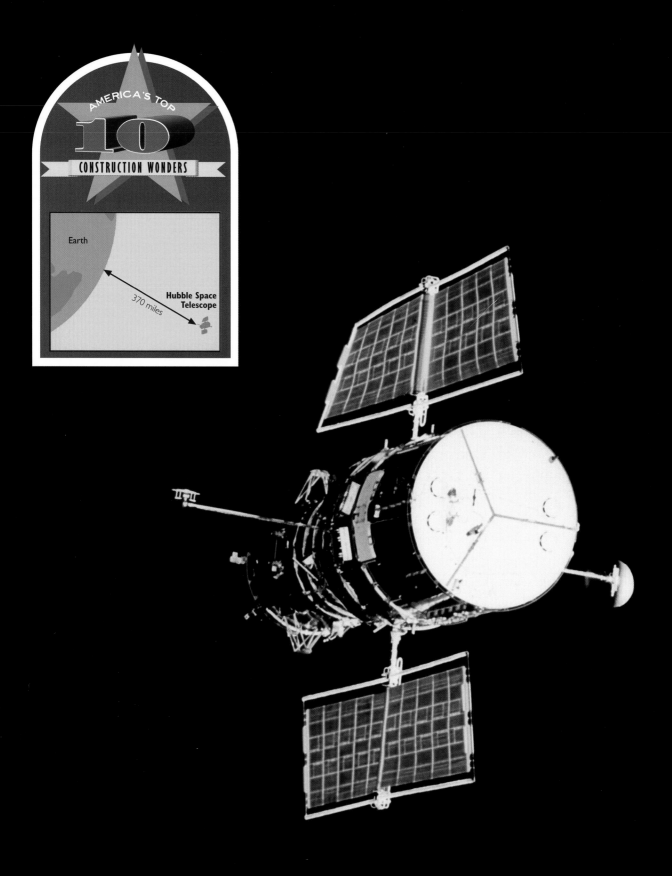

AMERICA'S TOP

10

CONSTRUCTION WONDERS

Earth

370 miles

Hubble Space
Telescope

The Hubble Space Telescope

In 1946, the astronomer Lyman Spitzer dreamed of building the first space platform that would circle the earth. It would be equipped with instruments for probing the universe. Spitzer's goal was to be able to view the skies without interference from the earth's atmosphere. The National Aeronautics and Space Administration (NASA) developed a design for the telescope, and in 1977 Congress approved the spending of federal money for the project. The telescope was named for Edwin Powell Hubble, the astronomer who found that there were galaxies beyond our own.

The Hubble Space Telescope, like many telescopes, uses mirrors to reflect light rays. The Hubble has an 8-foot primary, or main, mirror and a secondary mirror, which reflect light to various cameras and other instruments. The telescope is 4 stories tall. It is housed in an aluminum cylinder that is 14 feet wide and 43 feet long. Power is supplied by solar panels.

The Hubble was launched in April 1990. In June 1990, it began sending back its first, blurry pictures of space. This was happening because the primary mirror had been ground 10 thousandths of an inch too flat. In December 1993, the space shuttle *Endeavor* took 7 astronauts to repair the telescope. Billions of television viewers watched in amazement as they performed detailed work while floating in space. The astronauts succeeded in repairing the Hubble.

Since then, the Hubble Space Telescope has been sending remarkable images of objects in space back to Earth.

Launched: April 24, 1990
Height: 4 stories
Weight: More than 12 tons
Speed: 17,500 miles per hour
Cost: $1.5 billion
Fun fact: The "vision reach," or distance, the telescope can "see" is 12 billion miles.

Opposite page:
The Hubble Space Telescope transmits crystal-clear images of planets, galaxies, and other objects in space.

AMERICA'S TOP
10
CONSTRUCTION WONDERS

CANADA

VT ME
NH
NY MA
CT RI
PA
MD NJ Lincoln Tunnel

The Lincoln Tunnel

★ ★ ★ ★ ★ ★ ★ ★ ★ ★ ★ ★ ★ ★ ★

Named for Abraham Lincoln, the Lincoln Tunnel is the longest motor vehicle tunnel in America. In April 1930, studies were done on how to ease traffic between New York City's borough of Manhattan and the state of New Jersey. The Holland Tunnel already connected these 2 points, and it was decided that another tunnel was needed to link midtown Manhattan and New Jersey.

In 1934, work began on the project. Rock was blasted away from both sides of the Hudson as workers headed toward the river bottom. Next, a pre-made steel tunnel "shield" was inserted into the floor of the Hudson River, which took out chunks of the riverbed, allowing workers to move forward underneath the water.

Once it was finished, the hole for the tunnel was lined with concrete. Steel beams were then put in to support the roadway above. This left space for a fresh-air duct under the roadway. Air was drawn in from the outside and blown into the duct. Exhaust fans removed polluted air from the tunnel. In December 1937, the first of 3 tunnel tubes was ready, but completion of the project was delayed by problems. The roadways approaching the first tube had not been finished, which slowed approaching traffic. Fewer vehicles traveled through the tunnel than expected. As a result, fewer tolls were collected and lack of money became a problem. The third tube was not built until the mid-1950s. Today, the Lincoln Tunnel handles 40 million vehicles each year, making it the busiest tunnel in the United States.

Location: Between New York City and Weehauken, New Jersey
Opened: December 22, 1937
Length: 1.5 miles
Traffic: About 40 million vehicles per year
Cost: $75 million
Fun fact: 84 giant fans replace the air in the tunnel every 90 seconds.

Opposite page:
About 40 million cars drive through the Lincoln Tunnel every year.

AMERICA'S TOP
10
CONSTRUCTION WONDERS

AR

LA

TX

MS

Louisiana
Superdome

Louisiana Superdome

The Louisiana Superdome, in New Orleans, Louisiana, is the largest arena ever built. The stadium covers 13 acres and can hold up to 95,000 people.

The idea for the Superdome came from a New Orleans businessman named Dave Dixon, who wanted to bring professional football to the city. Construction began in August 1971, and the Superdome was opened 4 years later. Today, it is home to the New Orleans Saints football team. Several Super Bowl games have been held there, in addition to professional basketball, baseball, and gymnastics events.

Because New Orleans was built on what was once swampland, there were certain challenges to constructing the Superdome. For example, most stadiums have playing fields that are below street level. The Superdome's playing field, however, needed to be at street level so that it wouldn't become too damp. A complex system of columns and braces, and the domed roof, were needed to ensure the building's stability. The roof sits on a supporting structure called a tension ring. This ring rests on 96 columns arranged in a circle. The Superdome is shaped like a flying saucer. The walls hang from the roof, which is the largest steel dome in the world. The most exciting moment during construction of the arena was in 1973, when the temporary roof supports were removed. Everyone stopped working to see if the roof would be able to stand on its own! The roof held, and the Superdome was opened to the public in 1975, on August 3.

Location: New Orleans, Louisiana
Dedicated: August 3, 1975
Height: 27 stories
Diameter of dome: 680 feet
Interior space: 125 million cubic feet
Cost: $163 million
Fun fact: The dome contains 400 miles of electrical wiring.

Opposite page:
The Superdome rises 27 stories at its highest point.

AMERICA'S TOP

10

CONSTRUCTION WONDERS

WI

IA

Sears
Tower

MI

OH

IL

IN

MO

KY

The
Sears Tower

★ ★ ★ ★ ★ ★ ★ ★   ★ ★ ★ ★ ★ ★ ★ ★

The Sears Tower is the tallest building in America. By the late 1960s, the Sears Company had grown so large that it needed a new building for its 13,000 employees in the Chicago area. Some of the world's best engineers and architects were hired to work on the project.

Fazlur Khan, an engineer originally from Bangladesh, made it possible for the Sears Tower to reach its impressive height of 1,454 feet. Instead of using a traditional steel skeleton, he came up with a way to connect a series of tubes that were lighter and stronger. The diagonal supports for these tubes were designed to help the building withstand strong winds. Khan's design also used "setbacks" to increase the building's stability. As the building rose, each new level was set back from the level below, which made the Sears Tower resemble a staircase. The design of the project was so far ahead of its time that engineers thought robots would be able to deliver the mail—an interesting but unworkable idea!

Construction of the Sears Tower was dangerous. Workers scaled ropes and walked on narrow beams more than 1,000 feet above the ground. As the building grew in height, it took too much time for the construction workers to climb down for lunch, so kitchens were built on both the 33rd and 66th floors. On some days, high winds stopped construction.

In 1973, on May 3—just 3 years after the project was begun—the last beam was put into place. It was signed by 12,000 construction workers, Sears employees, and Chicago's mayor.

Location: Chicago, Illinois
Dedicated: May 3, 1973
Height: 1,454 feet
Weight: More than 222,500 tons
Engineer: Fazlur Khan
Architects: Skidmore, Owings, and Merrill
Number of stories: 110
Number of visitors: 1.5 million per year
Cost: More than $150 million
Fun fact: The tower contains 25,000 miles of plumbing pipe, 2,000 miles of electric wiring, and 145,000 light fixtures.

Opposite page:
The Sears Tower reaches the highest point in Chicago's skyline.

AMERICA'S TOP
10
CONSTRUCTION WONDERS

CANADA

Seattle
Space
Needle

WA

OR

ID

The
Seattle Space Needle

When the Seattle Space Needle was built for the 1962 World's Fair in Seattle, it was the tallest building west of the Mississippi River. The theme for the fair was science and technology. At the time, the Soviet launch of the first human-made satellite, *Sputnik*, had spurred the United States to join the "space race." Organizers of the fair thought that a space-aged structure would thus be a good centerpiece for the fair.

The first phase of construction involved excavation. At the end of 11 days, a 30-foot-deep hole covered the entire site. In order to stabilize the tall and slender Space Needle, the underground foundation had to weigh as much as the above-ground structure. To accomplish this, 250 tons of steel reinforcing bars and 72 anchor bolts were set into the hole before the concrete was poured. Then, in May, about 5,850 tons of concrete were poured for 12 straight hours.

Each of the steel beams made for the Space Needle was 90 feet long and weighed 27,000 pounds! To form the upper sections, which curve outward, the straight beams were heated and then bent. Once all the construction problems were solved, the Space Needle rose quickly. By September, it was 200 feet tall. The restaurant and observation decks, located more than 500 feet up from the ground, were completed in December. The last piece of steel added was the 50-foot torch tower. The Space Needle was the hit of the World's Fair. Almost 20,000 people rode its elevators every day to the observation level!

Location: Seattle, Washington
Dedicated: April 21, 1962
Height: 605 feet
Designer/Architects: John Ridley and Victor Steinbrueck
Number of visitors: 1.4 million visitors per year
Cost: About $4.5 million
Fun fact: It took 3,700 tons of steel to build the Space Needle.

Opposite page:
Today, the Space Needle
is the symbol of Seattle.

America's Top 10 Construction Wonders are not necessarily the largest, but at the time they were built, they were extraordinary engineering feats. Below is a list of 10 other notable construction projects.

More American Construction Wonders

Name, Location, *Description.*

Cathedral of St. John the Divine, New York City. *When finished, it will be the largest cathedral in the world.*

Golden Gate Bridge, San Francisco, California. *Second-longest bridge in America at 4,600 feet.*

Hoover Dam, Colorado, Arizona, Nevada. *Second-highest dam in America at 726 feet.*

Houston Astrodome, Houston, Texas. *First domed sports stadium.*

Mount Washington Cog Railway, the White Mountains, New Hampshire. *The first cog railway in America rises 3,625 feet.*

Oroville Dam, Feather, California. *Highest dam in America at 770 feet.*

Rockefeller Center, New York City. *Occupies more than 22 acres and has 19 buildings.*

Verrazano-Narrows Bridge, New York City. *Longest bridge in America at 4,260 feet.*

Washington Monument, Washington, D.C. *Tallest stone structure in the world at 555 feet.*

World Trade Center, New York City. *Second-tallest building in America at 1,377 feet.*

Glossary

anchor bolt A large bolt used to attach a structure to its foundation.

canal A human-made waterway.

conveyor A mechanical device for moving bulk material from place to place.

creeper derrick A piece of construction equipment that has a platform, crane, and a set of tracks. It is designed to climb the structure being built.

dam A structure built across a stream or river to hold back flowing water.

duct A tube, pipe, or channel.

engineer A person who designs buildings or large public works, such as bridges, dams, and canals.

excavation The process of removing by digging.

foundation The underlying part of a structure that supports its upper part.

lock A structure for lifting and lowering boats between the varying levels of a canal.

permafrost A permanently frozen layer below the earth's surface.

pipeline A line of welded pipe with valves and pumps that is used to transport liquids or gases.

skeleton A supporting framework or structure.

spillway A channel that allows excess water to run over or around an obstruction.

Further Reading

Aylesworth, Thomas and Virginia. *Chicago.* Woodbridge, CT: Blackbirch Press, 1990.

Boring, Mel. *Incredible Constructions and the People Who Built Them.* New York: Walker & Co., 1985.

Doherty, Craig and Katherine Doherty. *Building America: The Sears Tower.* Woodbridge, CT: Blackbirch Press, 1995.

———. *Building America: The Gateway Arch.* Woodbridge, CT: Blackbirch Press, 1995.

———. *Building America: The Seattle Space Needle*. Woodbridge, CT: Blackbirch Press, 1995.

———. *Building America: The Erie Canal*. Woodbridge, CT: Blackbirch Press, 1997.

Duncan, Michael. *How Skyscrapers Are Made*. New York: Facts On File, 1987.

Nirgiotis, Nicholas. *Erie Canal: Gateway to the West*. New York: Franklin Watts, 1993.

Ricciuti, Edward. *America's Top 10 Skyscrapers*. Woodbridge, CT: Blackbirch Press, 1997.

———. *America's Top 10 Bridges*. Woodbridge, CT: Blackbirch Press, 1997.

Stone, Tanya Lee. *America's Top 10 National Monuments*. Woodbridge, CT: Blackbirch Press, 1997.

Stein, R. Conrad. *The Story of the Erie Canal*. Chicago: Childrens Press, 1985.

Where to Get On-Line Information

Alaska Pipeline	http://www.apsc-taps.com/alyeska
Disney World's Epcot Center	http://www.disneypark.com
Gateway Arch	http://www.nps.gov/jeff/arch-home
Hubble Space Telescope	http://www.stsci.edu
Lincoln Tunnel	http://www.panynj.gov
Louisiana Superdome	http://www.superdome.com
Seattle Space Needle	http://www.spaceneedle.com

Index

Alaska, 3
Alaska Pipeline, 3
Alyeska Pipeline Service
   Company, 3
Appalachian Mountains, 7

Chicago, 19
Columbia River, 11
Crescent Bay Lake, 11

Disney World, 5
Dixon, Dave, 17

East Coast (U.S.), 7
Endeavor, 13
Epcot Center, 5
Erie Canal, 7
Experimental Prototype
   Community of Tomorrow.
   See Epcot Center.

Florida, 5
Future World, 5

Gateway Arch, 9
Grand Coulee, WA, 11
Grand Coulee Dam, 11

Hawley, Jesse, 7
Holland Tunnel, 15
Hubble, Edwin Powell, 13
Hubble Space Telescope, 13
Hudson River, 7, 15

Illinois, 19

Jefferson, Thomas, 9
Jefferson National Expansion
   Memorial. *See* Gateway
   Arch.

Khan, Fazlur, 19

Lake Erie, 7
Lincoln, Abraham, 15
Lincoln Tunnel, 15
Lockport, NY, 7
Louisiana, 17
Louisiana Superdome, 17

Manhattan, 15
Mississippi River, 9
Missouri, 9

National Aeronautics and
   Space Administration
   (NASA), 13
New Jersey, 15
New Orleans, 17
New Orleans Saints, 17

New York, 7, 11
New York City, 7, 11

Permafrost, 3
Prudhoe Bay, 3

Ridley, John, 21
Rome, NY, 7

Saarinen, Eero, 9

St. Louis, 9
Sears Company, 19
Sears Tower, 19
Seattle, 21
Skidmore, Owings, and
    Merrill (architects), 19
Smith, Luther Ely, 9
"Space race," 21
Spaceship Earth, 5
Spitzer, Lyman, 13
Sputnik, 21

Steinbrueck, Victor, 21
Super Bowl, 17

Valdez, 3

Washington, 11, 19
Weehauken, NJ, 15
World Showcase, 5
World War II, 9
World's Fair (1962), 21

Photo Credits

Cover and page 2: Courtesy of Alyeska Pipeline Service Company; cover and page 4: ©Steve Vidler/Leo de Wys, Inc.; cover and page 6: New York State Thruway Authority; cover and page 8: Courtesy of the St. Louis Convention and Visitors Commission; cover and page 10: United States Department of the Interior/Bureau of Reclamation; cover and page 12: Courtesy of NASA; cover and page 14: Port Authority of New York and New Jersey; cover and page 16: Louisiana Office of Tourism; cover and page 18: ©Joseph Nettis/Photo Researchers, Inc.; cover and page 20: Courtesy of Space Needle Corporation.